Little Yoga

This Little Yoga book
belongs to

. . . .

For scarlett with love — R. W.

For my granddaughter Mathilda — M. S.

Henry Holt and Company
Publishers since 1866
175 Fifth Avenue
New York, NY 10010
mackids.com

First published in the United States in 2005 by Henry Holt and Company
Simultaneously published in the United Kingdom in 2005 by Random House Children's Books

Library of Congress Cataloging-in-Publication Data
Whitford, Rebecca.
Little yoga: a toddler's first book of yoga / Rebecca Whitford & Martina Selway.—1st American ed.
p.   cm.
ISBN 978-0-8050-7879-4
1. Hatha yoga for children—Juvenile literature. 2. Hatha yoga—Juvenile literature.
I. Selway, Martina. II. Title.
RJ133.7.W48 2005   613.7'046'083—dc22   2004024280

First American Edition—2005
Printed in China
15 17 19 20 18 16 14

Little Yoga

A Toddler's First Book of Yoga

Rebecca Whitford & Martina Selway

HENRY HOLT AND COMPANY
NEW YORK

Yoga Baby—

spreads his arms like a

flutter
flutter

butterfly.

hangs down like a

oooh
oooh

monkey.

Yoga Baby

breathes like a

haaaaa

haaaaa

lion—haaaa.

Yoga Baby—

stretches her back like a

meow meow

cat.

Yoga Baby—

wags his tail like a

woof
woof

dog.

Yoga Baby—

curls up like a

ZZZZZZZ
ZZZZZZZ

sleeping mouse.

wobbles like a

tweet tweet

little bird.

Yoga Baby—

crouches like a

ribbit
ribbit

frog.

Yoga Baby

says, Time for a

Z Z Z Z

rest—

z z z z z z z z

ahh, shh, shh.

A Note to Parents and Caregivers

Little Yoga is a gentle introduction to a balanced yoga sequence for toddlers to enjoy—either by copying Yoga Baby and practicing with Mom or Dad or to simply read and share. Yoga is a great way for children to develop strength and suppleness, improve physical coordination and mental concentration, and increase self-awareness and self-confidence. With practice, yoga can help to calm and relax toddlers by encouraging moments of quiet and stillness.

Toddlers are naturally flexible and will enjoy the animal role-play but may find balancing and relaxing more challenging. *Little Yoga* is designed for fun, not as a manual, so allow it to take its own playful form and be sure to give your child lots of encouragement.

Practice Tips

- Practice with bare feet on a nonslip surface; use a clear space in a warm room and wear loose, comfortable clothing.

- As with any form of exercise, it is best not to practice this sequence immediately after eating.

- Practice with your child so that he or she can copy you.

- Use your own judgment about your child's ability and let your child move at his or her own pace, giving support where necessary.

- Encourage your child to try poses but do not look for or expect perfection. Most of all *Little Yoga* is meant to be an enjoyable, positive experience.

- Don't force your toddler into a pose or let him or her hold any pose for too long.

- Allow your child to play with a pose before moving on to the next one.

- Encourage your child to keep his or her breath flowing—toddlers are too young to practice controlled breathing—and to move slowly in and out of the poses.

- Discourage your child from putting weight onto his or her head (they are tempted to do this in the Downward Dog pose) and be ready to catch your Yoga Baby when balancing!

- Simple stories can help your Yoga Baby relax when in the resting pose.

- The photos that follow are not precise because they are a real reflection of how our toddlers have interpreted the poses.

Most important, keep your *Little Yoga* practice **simple** and **playful!**

Butterfly (Flying Eagle)

Monkey (Forward Bend)

a) Cat

Lion (Lion Breath)

b) Cat

Dog (Downward Dog)

Bird (Tree Balance)

Mouse (Child's Pose)

Frog (Squat)

Rest (Savasana)

Explanation of Poses

Butterfly (Flying Eagle)—from a standing position raise arms out and up. Stretch up while rising on tiptoes. Lower arms to the sides and come down slowly onto heels. It may help to practice arm movements before trying tiptoes.

Monkey (Forward Bend)—from a standing position raise arms in front, then bend from the waist, letting upper body, arms, and hands relax toward the floor. Keep knees bent if more comfortable. Uncurl slowly back to a standing position.

Lion (Lion Breath)—start in a cross-legged, straight-backed sitting position with hands resting on knees. Breathe in, then breathe out with a loud *haaa* sound while sticking the tongue out as far as possible and stretching arms out in front with fingers spread. Some toddlers can also look up to the space between their eyebrows!

Cat—on hands and knees, with knees directly under hips, feet parallel, and wrists directly under shoulders, tilt the pelvis while moving the chest out, lifting the chin, and looking up. Then reverse directions: tuck bottom in, arch the back so that it is rounded, and relax the head. Repeat both parts of the pose as a continuous movement.

Dog (Downward Dog)—on hands and knees, tuck toes under onto the floor. Lift hips and bottom up, push heels down toward the floor, push away from floor with the palms, and relax the head and neck. Return to starting position.

Mouse (Child's Pose)—from all fours, put legs together and sink hips/bottom back toward the feet, forehead to the floor. Try to keep spine in a straight line. Lay arms alongside legs and turn the palms up. Hold and relax.

Bird (Tree Balance)—from standing, shift weight onto left leg. Raise right heel to rest on left ankle, toes on the floor and right knee out to the side. Bring hands into prayer position in front of chest. When balanced, lift hands in prayer position above head and stretch up. Lower arms to prayer position at chest height and release hands to sides. Bring foot to the floor. Repeat on the other side. It helps to practice against a wall. Once balanced it may be possible to bring the foot farther up the inside of the leg, keeping the knee out to the side.

Frog (Squat)—stand with feet at least hip-width apart, toes turned out. Squat down, putting hands on the floor between the knees, directly under the shoulders. Try to keep a straight spine with head and spine in line.

Rest (Savasana)—lie down on back, keeping body in a straight line. Have legs hip-width apart and let feet relax out to the sides. Keep arms away from the body and palms turned up. Try to keep head in line with the spine. Close the eyes. Imagine sinking into a cloud. . . .